ALL AROUND THE WORLD
POLAND

by Kristine Spanier, MLIS

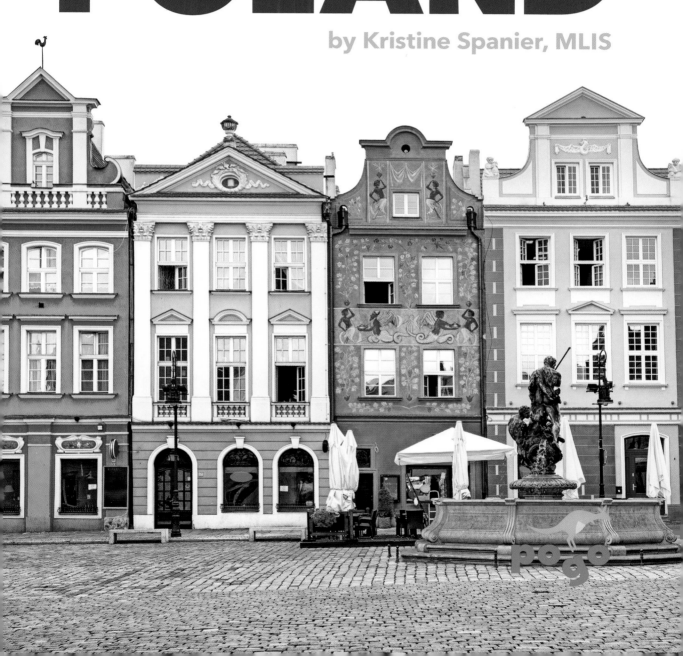

Ideas for Parents and Teachers

Pogo Books let children practice reading informational text while introducing them to nonfiction features such as headings, labels, sidebars, maps, and diagrams, as well as a table of contents, glossary, and index.

Carefully leveled text with a strong photo match offers early fluent readers the support they need to succeed.

Before Reading

- "Walk" through the book and point out the various nonfiction features. Ask the student what purpose each feature serves.
- Look at the glossary together. Read and discuss the words.

Read the Book

- Have the child read the book independently.
- Invite him or her to list questions that arise from reading.

After Reading

- Discuss the child's questions. Talk about how he or she might find answers to those questions.
- Prompt the child to think more. Ask: Poland's people do different activities depending on the season. Does the climate affect what you do for fun where you live?

Pogo Books are published by Jump!
5357 Penn Avenue South
Minneapolis, MN 55419
www.jumplibrary.com

Library of Congress Cataloging-in-Publication Data

Names: Spanier, Kristine, author.
Title: Poland / by Kristine Spanier.
Description: Minneapolis, MN: Jump!, [2021]
Series: All around the world | Includes index.
Audience: Ages 7-10 | Audience: Grades 2-3
Identifiers: LCCN 2019047572 (print)
LCCN 2019047573 (ebook)
ISBN 9781645273509 (hardcover)
ISBN 9781645273516 (paperback)
ISBN 9781645273523 (ebook)
Subjects: LCSH: Poland—Juvenile literature.
Classification: LCC DK4147 .S63 2021 (print)
LCC DK4147 (ebook) | DDC 943.8—dc23
LC record available at https://lccn.loc.gov/2019047572
LC ebook record available at https://lccn.loc.gov/2019047573

Editor: Jenna Gleisner
Designer: Molly Ballanger

Photo Credits: darrro/iStock, cover; Boris Stroujko/Shutterstock, 1; Pixfiction/Shutterstock, 3; ewg3D/iStock, 4; Janusz Lipinski/Shutterstock, 5; JaroPienza/iStock, 6-7; PocholoCalapre/iStock, 8-9; volkova natalia/Shutterstock, 10; imageBROKER.com/Shutterstock, 11; Artur Gazda/iStock, 12-13; Alla Pogrebnaya/Shutterstock, 14; Stock Connection/SuperStock, 15; freeskyline/iStock, 16-17l; Dar1930/iStock, 16-17tr; gkrphoto/Shutterstock, 16-17br; KatarzynaBialasiewicz/iStock, 18-19; BeeZeePhoto/Shutterstock, 20-21; JGA/Shutterstock, 23.

Printed in the United States of America at Corporate Graphics in North Mankato, Minnesota.

TABLE OF CONTENTS

CHAPTER 1

WELCOME TO POLAND!

Would you like to see Malbork Castle? This was a **fortress** in the 1200s! Now you can visit and see it!

Malbork Castle

Or would you like to swim in a lake? Almost 10,000 lakes are here! Welcome to Poland!

Wieliczka
Salt Mine

Salt **mines** have been here since the 1200s. Rock salt was mined until the late 1900s. See statues and decorations in the mines. They are made of salt!

Warsaw is the **capital**. This city was destroyed in World War II (1939–1945). People here have **restored** it.

The **president** represents the country at events. The president also chooses a **prime minister**. This person leads the government.

DID YOU KNOW?

German **Nazis** took over Poland during World War II. Auschwitz is near Kraków. It was the largest **concentration camp** in Europe. It is now a **memorial**.

Warsaw

CHAPTER 2

ANIMALS AND LAND

Beautiful forests cover parts of this country. Deer and wild pigs live in them. European bison can be found in the Bialowieza Forest.

European bison

white stork

Brown bears make their home in the Carpathian Mountains. White storks live in Zywkowo. More than 15,000 **migrate** here every summer!

The Oder River reaches the Baltic Sea. It is used for shipping. Szczecin is a **port** city on this river.

WHAT DO YOU THINK?

Polish **exports** include coal and many **crops**. Rye and potatoes are a couple. Beef cattle, dairy cows, and pigs are raised on farms here, too. What crops or animals are raised near you?

Szczecin

Oder River

CHAPTER 3

PEOPLE IN POLAND

Summer months are warm. People enjoy the beach! They might go skimboarding in the ocean. This is like surfing.

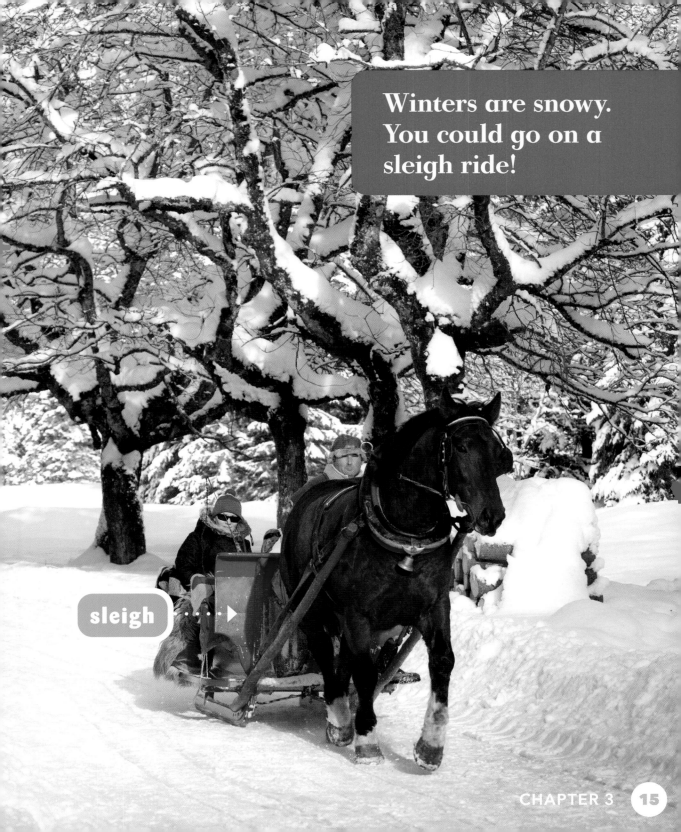

Winters are snowy. You could go on a sleigh ride!

sleigh ·····▶

Would you like to try pierogi? These are dumplings. Uszka are like ravioli. They are sometimes served in beet soup. How about a bowl of czarnina? It is duck soup! Fresh bread is eaten every day.

pierogi

czarnina

uszka

Children start school when they are seven years old. They go until they are 18. Some students take part in green schools. They learn about protecting the **environment**. Students might go to three years of high school. Or they go to a school for two years for job training.

WHAT DO YOU THINK?

Protecting the environment is important to Poland's people. What do you do to help protect Earth?

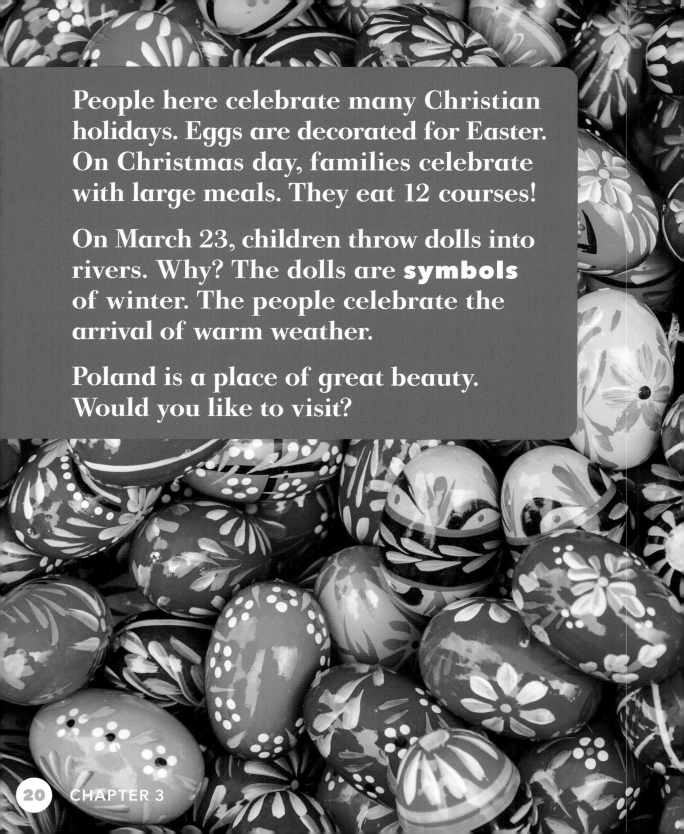

People here celebrate many Christian holidays. Eggs are decorated for Easter. On Christmas day, families celebrate with large meals. They eat 12 courses!

On March 23, children throw dolls into rivers. Why? The dolls are **symbols** of winter. The people celebrate the arrival of warm weather.

Poland is a place of great beauty. Would you like to visit?

TAKE A LOOK!

Many Polish families fill Easter baskets with special foods, decorated eggs, and a candle. They take them to church to be blessed. On Easter, they feast on the foods.

BREAD

CHEESE

HAM

BACON

SAUSAGE

EGGS

BUTTER

SALT

CANDLE

QUICK FACTS & TOOLS

POLAND

Location: central Europe

Size: 120,728 square miles (312,684 square kilometers)

Population: 38,420,687 (July 2018 estimate)

Capital: Warsaw

Type of Government: parliamentary republic

Language: Polish

Exports: coal, machinery and transport equipment, manufactured goods

Currency: Polish złoty

capital: A city where government leaders meet.

concentration camp: A place where large numbers of political prisoners are detained under armed guard.

crops: Plants grown for food.

environment: The natural surroundings of living things, such as the air, land, or sea.

exports: Products sold to different countries.

fortress: A place that is fortified against attack.

memorial: Something that is built, such as a statue or monument, to help people remember a person or event.

migrate: To move to another area or climate at a particular time of year.

mines: Pits or holes in Earth from which mineral substances are taken.

Nazis: Members of a German fascist party that controlled Germany from 1933 to 1945 under Adolf Hitler.

port: A town or city with a harbor where ships can load and unload goods.

president: A leader of a country, sometimes in a ceremonial position.

prime minister: The leader of a country.

restored: Brought back to an original condition.

symbols: Objects or designs that stand for, suggest, or represent something else.

Poland's currency

INDEX

TO LEARN MORE

Finding more information is as easy as 1, 2, 3.

❶ **Go to www.factsurfer.com**

❷ **Enter "Poland" into the search box.**

❸ **Click the "Surf" button to see a list of websites.**

FACT SURFER